# EDINBURGH
## THROUGH THE
# LENS

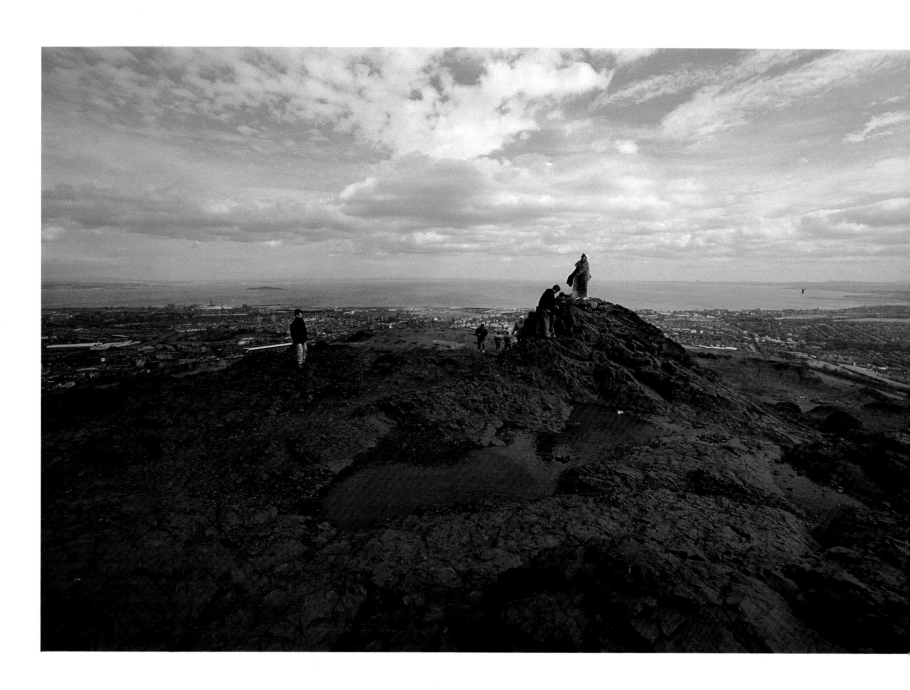

# EDINBURGH
## THROUGH THE
# LENS

## IAN TORRANCE

*Foreword by the*

### Rt. Hon. Eleanor McLaughlin

*Lord Provost of Edinburgh*

## JOHN DONALD PUBLISHERS

*EDINBURGH*

# PREFACE

EDINBURGH IS A FEAST for the eyes at every turn. So it was
a pleasure to be asked to produce this photographic
tribute to what is undoubtedly one of the most
beautiful capitals in the world.

The Old Town and New Town are of course
famous – one crowded, romantic and filled with
history, the other spacious, elegant and a major
financial centre. But there is the wider scene as well,
from the Pentland Hills to the docks at Leith, from
Cramond to Portobello. And not least there is
Holyrood Park. I feel you could walk here daily and
always find something new to photograph. How
fortunate we are to have such natural beauty, and
grandeur too in Arthur's Seat, on our own doorstep.

Above all there are the people, without whom
Edinburgh simply wouldn't be the Edinburgh we
know. With the passing seasons and under changing
skies, they're the final and the vital element that brings
the streets to life.

Through my lens, I have tried to capture
something of all of this, and to share with you the
unique experience that is Edinburgh.

IAN TORRANCE

My thanks go to the National Gallery of Scotland, the
Scottish Record Office, and the Signet Library for their
assistance in the preparation of this book.

*Dedication*

To my wife and family who have put
up with my sudden vanishing acts, to
that Great Photographer in the Sky
who keeps pointing me in the right
direction, and to the people of
Edinburgh who helped make the book
possible.

ISBN 0 85976 322 6

# FOREWORD

I WAS DELIGHTED to be asked to write a Foreword for this book 'Edinburgh Through The Lens'. As a native of this great city of Edinburgh, I welcome this beautiful collection of photographs by another native, Ian Torrance.

Besides being a master of his craft, Ian knows his Edinburgh intimately, and this is what makes his book a unique record; a combination of superb skill and acute observation.

The most important aspect of a city are the people, both the people of Edinburgh and of course the many visitors who come to us all year round – not just the buildings and the scenery. One after another, moments are captured: happy ones, tender ones, humorous ones, fleeting ones. The people are shown unselfconsciously at work and at play, and in the unrivalled environment that is Edinburgh, Edinburgh throughout the year in all her changing moods.

This will be a book to keep and treasure, and I am very happy to recommend it.

RT. HON ELEANOR McLAUGHLIN
*LORD PROVOST OF EDINBURGH*

1. Seen from Corstorphine Hill, a steepled Edinburgh rises out of January mists. Beyond the Castle lie the Pentland Hills, and in front of it are the triple spires of St. Mary's Cathedral.

2. Springtime, and a young girl enjoys the daffodils in Princes Street Gardens.

3. Autumn sunlight filters through the smoke from burning leaves in New Town Gardens between Royal Circus and India Place.

4. Dappled October sunlight enhances the elegant symmetry – spoiled only by some necessary window cleaning – of Belgrave Crescent near the Dean Bridge.

5. A new view of the Bank of Scotland building at the top of the Mound – reflected this time on a rainy platform at Waverley Station.

6. Magic September moment for a young woman in Inverleith Park.

8. . . . and over in George Street in the New Town, the world goes about its business.

7. A Grassmarket worthy. It's May, and weather to sit out again . . . and watch the world go by.

9. An evening to remember. Maytime, and Edinburgh spreads itself in all its glory before this young couple as they watch the sun go down over the Forth.

10. May blossoms all round as youngsters take a walk in Northfield.

11. History comes to life for a school class visiting the Canongate Kirk in the Royal Mile.

12. It's a dog's life . . . in the Water of Leith near St. Bernard's Well.

13. . . . tied to the traffic lights outside the pub. In this case master is visiting the King's Wark in Leith.

14. . . . waiting for owner at Broughton Supermarket.

15. Waverley Market Shopping Centre, and it's time to cut the rooftop grass.

16. A family at play in the foreground while others enjoy the sunshine on the benches in Princes Street Gardens.

17. Princes Street Gardens again, and this time two tourists are trying to photograph one of the resident squirrels.

18. A summer visitor enjoys the evening sun on the Monument on Calton Hill.

19. The closes or narrow passages of the Old Town are one of its perpetual sources of surprise and delight. This is Lady Stair's Close, leading from the Lawnmarket to the Mound. To the left, Lady Stair's House is a museum to Burns, Scott and Stevenson.

20. Another close . . . this time the Vennel, leading down past the Flodden Wall to the Grassmarket with the Castle's Half-Moon Battery beyond.

21. Advocates Close off the Royal Mile provides this sudden view of the Scott Monument down on Princes Street.

22. Waverley Station, and time for a chat as travellers hurry by.

23. Schoolchildren take a break in Princes Street Gardens. One youngster smacks her lips over a particularly good packed lunch.

24. More serious business this time. Another class pays an educational visit to the National Gallery.

25. No, not saving the world . . . just urging you to go and buy a suit. Summer in George Street.

27. Sunset at Cramond. A swan admires its own reflection.

26. Spring is coming on again, and it's time to admire the crocuses at the foot of Playfair Steps. Beyond, beside the National Gallery, a street musician braves the elements.

28. More evening effects. Here are the monuments on Calton Hill silhouetted against the Forth. A view from Arthur's Seat.

30. The setting sun hits Portobello Beach.

29. Late evening bus queue at Craigmillar.

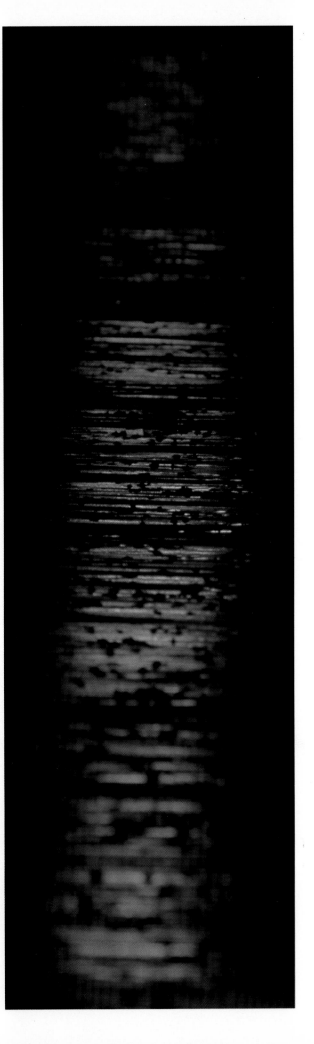

31. Edinburgh seen through December mists. The nearest buildings are the student residences at Pollock Halls by the Commonwealth Pool.

32. Early morning exercise on Portobello Beach in February for horses, dog and riders.

33. Strange effects at 6 a.m. Rain dries out on a George Street pavement.

34. Holyrood Park, a great place to walk the dogs.

35. Suburban cornfields with the Pentland Hills beyond.

36. A mural on a tenement wall depicts life in Leith. This is at the foot of Ferry Road where it joins North Junction Street.

37. Sunset framed by Leith Docks cranes.

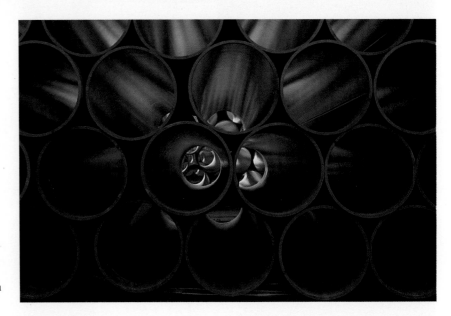

38. Patterns of light play on oil pipes in storage at Leith Docks.

39. Spring sunlight, and a woman walks down the steps of the Vennel to the Grassmarket.

40. Time for a break, at the West Bow Well in the Grassmarket.

41. Big boats . . .

42. . . . and little boats.

43. Time for a coffee in Debenhams, and a splendid view of the Castle.

44. Time for a bite on Students Day Parade.

45. Just arrived – a tourist at Waverley Station.

46. Lucky white heather? Heather seller near the Castle.

47. Making music for shoppers in Princes Street.

49. Relaxing in a Frederick Street restaurant after a hard day's tourism.

48. Residences at the top of the Mound, and a girl student takes advantage of the sun.

50. Tourists near John Knox's House take to the kerb to enjoy their ice-creams.

51. A drink in the open air at the Green Tree in the Cowgate.

52. Pot plants make a brave show in South Gray's Close. Just goes to show how you can modernise an old close without spoiling it.

53. A football match in Inverleith Park, and wherever you go the Castle's always there.

54. Scenes at a Meadows Fair – a balloon girl tucks into a hamburger.

55. An aspiring baseball player practises hard.

56. A trick cyclist delights the crowd.

57. Balletic grace on a skateboard.

58. As spectacular a scene as you'll see in any city. It's springtime, and as the sun goes down, late evening strollers are dramatically silhouetted against a glowing sky.

59. Young love finds a perfect setting at Newhaven Harbour.

60. A breathtaking sunset as a tanker plies the Forth, photographed from Arthur's Seat.

61. Sharp winter light outlines a mother and child as they feed the ducks on the Union Canal near Harrison Park.

62. Swans and ducks abound on the wintery waters of St. Margaret's Loch, Holyrood Park.

63. A nostalgic stroll through the dock area at Leith.

64. As evening draws on, a couple on the Crags seem almost suspended over the city's northern skyline.

65. Promenade time for toddlers.

66. Curving patterns set off this tranquil autumn scene by the boating pond in Inverleith.

67. Railway line, viaduct and canal at Longstone point dramatically towards the distant Castle.

68. Playtime with pigeons.

69. Strumming away on the Mound – it's hair-raising!

70. Putting heart and soul into it.

71. Greyfriars Bobby makes the perfect spot to snap the family pet.

72. A cannon on the Castle ramparts makes for an exciting family photograph.

73. Edinburgh Castle still has its garrison.

74. Students' Charities Day. Trapeze act outside the Royal Scottish Academy.

75. Say cheese! Tourists pose outside Holyrood Palace.

76. A visitor wants to see what's outside John Knox's House as well as in.

77. Time to reflect before the music starts.

78. Street musician outside the National Gallery. Shoppers from Princes Street make for Playfair Steps and the Mound.

79. Peace and quiet for a girl to study among the
tombstones in Greyfriars Churchyard.

80. Locals take the sun outside the Canongate Kirk.

81. . . . and the sun reaches into the cloistered calm of the Lower Signet Library.

83. Washing day, with flowers, at Portsburgh Square in the Old Town.

82. The all-too familiar figure of the traffic warden.

84. In the Botanic Gardens.

85. Young tourist in the Old Town.

86. On a day like this, what better place to read the morning paper than Arthur's Seat?

87. Don't look now but . . . geese follow a young walker in Holyrood Park.

88. Waterfall at Cramond.

89. Young lad with boat in Inverleith Park.

90. Chapel Wynd at the Old Town's West Port. The Castle provides the ever-present backdrop.

91. The Castle is backdrop yet again for a family snapshot.

92. Setting off on the ever popular ghost tour of the closes of the Old Town.

93. December sky, seen from Calton Hill and looking towards Princes Street.

94. The sun's rays transform the clock tower of the North British Hotel which was still being refurbished when this shot was taken, showing the

95. A walker braves a threatening winter sky on Calton Hill.

96. Evening strollers etched against the sands at Portobello.

97. December fog hangs over the city but Salisbury Crags and Arthur's Seat rise above it all. In the foreground hardy golfers brave conditions on the Braids.

98. Light catches the railway lines at Waverley Station. Behind are the arches of North Bridge.

99. A different form of transport approaches Queen Street.

100. Heriot Row in the New Town, looking smart in crisp sunlight.

101. Newly planted trees will enhance Leith Walk.

102. Happiness is . . . an ice-cream
cone

103. . . . or a chat with a loved one.

104. Beating Retreat at Holyrood Palace. The occasion is the General Assembly of the Church of Scotland in May.

105. A piper plays for tourists on 'The Royal Scotsman' before it leaves on its Scottish tour from Waverley Station.

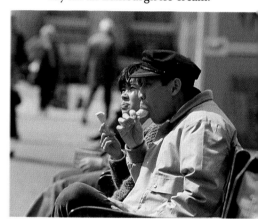

107. Some people will come a long way for an Edinburgh ice-cream.

106. Free classical concert is particularly enjoyed by one passer by as he decides to take a rest.

108. Enjoying Scotland's Other National Drink.

109. The traditional skills of the stonemason survive in Edinburgh.

110. A pavement artist displays different skills outside the Royal Scottish Academy.

111. Early Sunday morning on the Royal Mile. In the foreground the Tron Kirk, and up the hill the crown of St. Giles'.

112. The locals go about their business as restoration work continues in the High Street.

113. A Castle sentry stands impassive as young tourists struggle with their camera.

114. Youngsters play in Holyrood Park. Behind them the Radical Road snakes its way up and around the Crags.

115. Time for a bath – in Dunsapie Loch.

116. A panorama from Salisbury Crags. Smoke drifts lazily towards the Pentlands.

117. Dunsapie Loch in Holyrood Park. A wonderful spot for city dwellers to relax.

118. The infamous history of Deacon Brodie, one of Edinburgh's most colourful rogues, told on the wall of the Lawnmarket pub that bears his name.

119. Let's go in here, honey! A tourist waves from the steps of John Knox's House.

120. Dressed for the weather in High Street. Yes, it does sometimes rain in Edinburgh.

121. Stop! A policeman clears the way for dignitaries in canny procession from the Church of Scotland General Assembly to the Free Church Assembly over the way.

122. The latest in fashion, and the traditional ice-cream too!

123. "Excuse me, sir. I think this instrument's melted." But help is at hand for thirsty Grassmarket jazz musicians.

124. Not quite a hundred and one trombones, but you're never too young to join in.

125. An unusual view of the Grassmarket – reflected in brass.

126. Hoots mon! Jazz goes tartan.

127. Modern sheltered housing. Fountain Court, off Hyndfords Close behind the High Street.

128. A wee dog stands guard outside aptly named Blackie House.

129. A young visitor joins the
cartoon penguins at Edinburgh Zoo.

130. Edinburgh Zoo again, and
penguins (real ones this time) parade
before a rapt audience.

131. Cats come out to play in Websters Land near the Grassmarket.

132. Wheels upon wheels near the National Library on George IV Bridge.

133. . . . and if you don't have a bicycle, there's always an alternative.

134. Not the Sahara, but Portobello Beach, and a mother and daughter caught in a sandstorm.

135. Bowling on the Royal Mile?
Whatever next! An all-weather green
near Whiteford House.

136. Dressing up is always fun!
Especially on a wall in the
Grassmarket.

137. Princes Street traffic weaves an early evening spell.

138. Twilight comes to Edinburgh's countryside near Craigmillar Castle.

140 (overleaf). The Glenlivet Fireworks Concert, one of the most spectacular features of the Edinburgh Festival, brings magic to Edinburgh's skyline.

139. . . . and to the head office of the Bank of Scotland at the top of the Mound.

141. Mist-shrouded Prestonfield
House on a cold December morning.

142. . . . and the mists clear to reveal
the Royal Scots Greys' proud
memorial in Princes Street.

143. The pinnacled splendour of Fettes College, Edinburgh's famous public school.

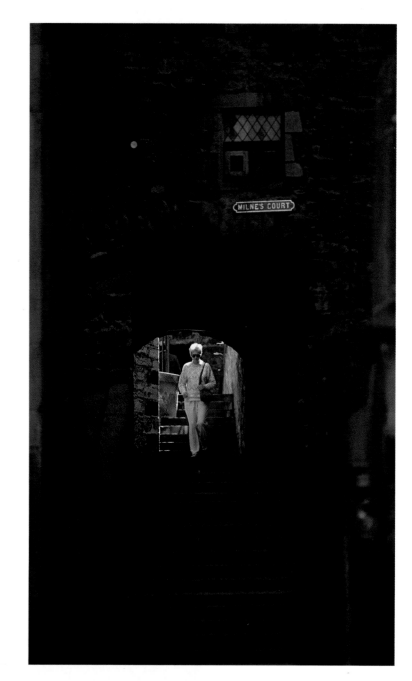

144. A room with a view. This one's in the Old Town's Grassmarket.

145 (above right). The Old Town again. This time a study in light and shadow at Milne's Court.

146. An audience for the Polar bears at the Zoo.

147. Trim new chimney pots direct this rooftop view towards the New Town.

148. Late for work? A quick dash from Haymarket Station.

149. Relaxing under Salisbury Crags.

150. Two-way transport can come in handy in Edinburgh.

151. American football comes to town. In the background the good old Scottish version goes on as it always will.

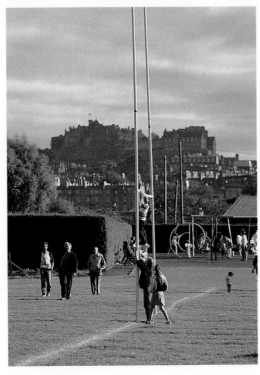

152. The Castle from Inverleith Park. Rugby posts can serve more than one purpose.

154. Putting suddenly takes a back seat in Princes Street Gardens.

153. Autumn tints. Two youngsters stride through the fallen leaves.

155. Festival flags are out as crowds throng to the Military Tattoo on the Castle Esplanade.

156. A more peaceful scene, taken from Calton Hill, as the sun goes down behind the crown of St. Giles' on the High Street.

157. The Castle seen from Holyrood Park. The spire is that of the former Highland Tolbooth Church at the head of the Lawnmarket.

158. In the Botanic Gardens. An artist studies the colours.

159. I see no ships . . . young tourist at the Castle.

160. Light and shadow in Whitehorse Close, a former coaching inn, at the foot of the Canongate.

161. All the joy of the Jazz Festival is there to see.

163. Tourist at work.

162. Queuing for a pint before a Rugby International.

164. A view, in typical pearly light, of the National Gallery with the Royal Scottish Academy beyond.

165. Rich reflections among the Old Masters in the National Gallery.

166. Greeting May Day from Edinburgh's highest spot, the top of Arthur's Seat.

167. A May Day ritual – washing your face in the early morning dew.

168. The May Day sun shares its glory with everyone and every thing.

169. Jogging on a frosty morning in Holyrood Park. A marvellous place to do it.

170. A stylish wedding photo in Holyrood Park.

171. A robotic dancer intrigues crowds at the Mound.

172. . . . but even robots take a rest, this time on the steps of the Royal Scottish Academy.

174. Happy times at the bric-a-brac stall.

173. No nuts in an Aero bar.

175. A walk on the sands at Portobello to blow the cobwebs away.

176. A time to relax – Edinburgh University graduates leave the McEwan Hall after receiving their degrees.

177. A graduate holds aloft his well-earned scroll.

178. Congratulations from an unusual quarter.

179. Shades of Auld Reekie . . . a
man walks his dog in Holyrood Park
as the Castle breaks through early
mist.

180. Before the Scotland-England encounter at Murrayfield. Is he rubbing his hands at the prospect of a Scotland victory, or in anticipation of a good day's takings?

181. For those who didn't get into Murrayfield, it's a case of all eyes on the TV in a pub nearby.

182. Ready for the Auld Enemy.

183. On their knees – a plea for the precious tickets.

184. Seconds from the final whistle at Murrayfield. The crowd still a study in concentration, but a solitary Scots flag signals the jubilation to come. Scotland will win the lot – Grand Slam, Triple Crown, and Calcutta Cup.

185. A touch of paint on the Fringe.

186. Edinburgh, the windy city.

187. Meadowbank Stadium, the day after the big athletics event. One young lad imagines his moment of triumph.

188. Autumn
comes to Princes
Street Gardens.

189. Early morning sweeper in Rose Street while workers and tourists are still abed.

191. January snow on the high ground of Lothianburn Golf Course – a great chance for the kids to sledge.

190. A heavy early morning frost fails to deter golfers at Prestonfield.

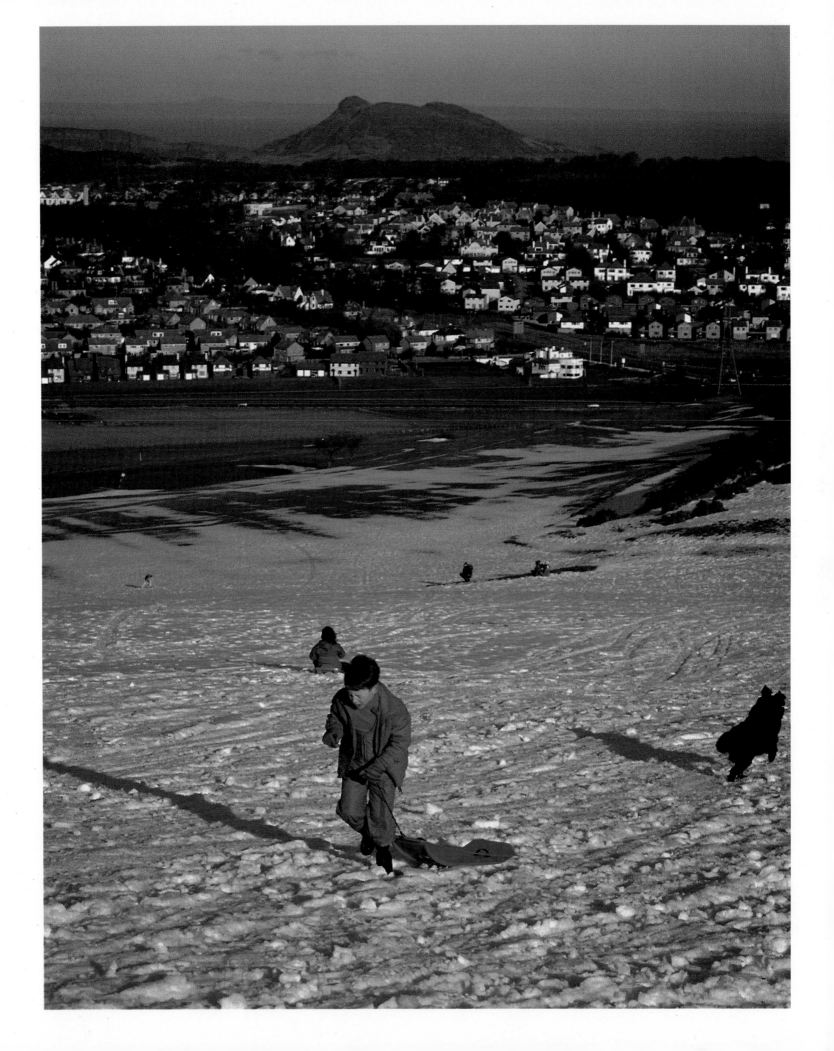

192. The building trade joins in the Christmas spirit at Picardy Place.

193. Christmas comes to George Street.

194. No tourists now! A light fall of snow in Princes Street.

195. Castle and Salisbury Crags still assert themselves through the cloud.

196. The Royal Company of Archers, the Queen's Bodyguard for Scotland, on duty at the Garden Party in Holyrood Palace.

197. An informal moment before the ceremonial.

198. The Royal Garden Party in progress.
A view from Salisbury Crags.

199. Hold on to your hats – guests arrive
for the Garden Party.

200 & 201. Everyone's favourite, especially the photographers'. The Queen Mother in her 90th year attends the Royal Garden Party.

202. The sun goes down in
splendour over Edinburgh.

203. Souvenir seller at the foot of the
Mound. Who would disagree?